FLIGHT FEATHERS

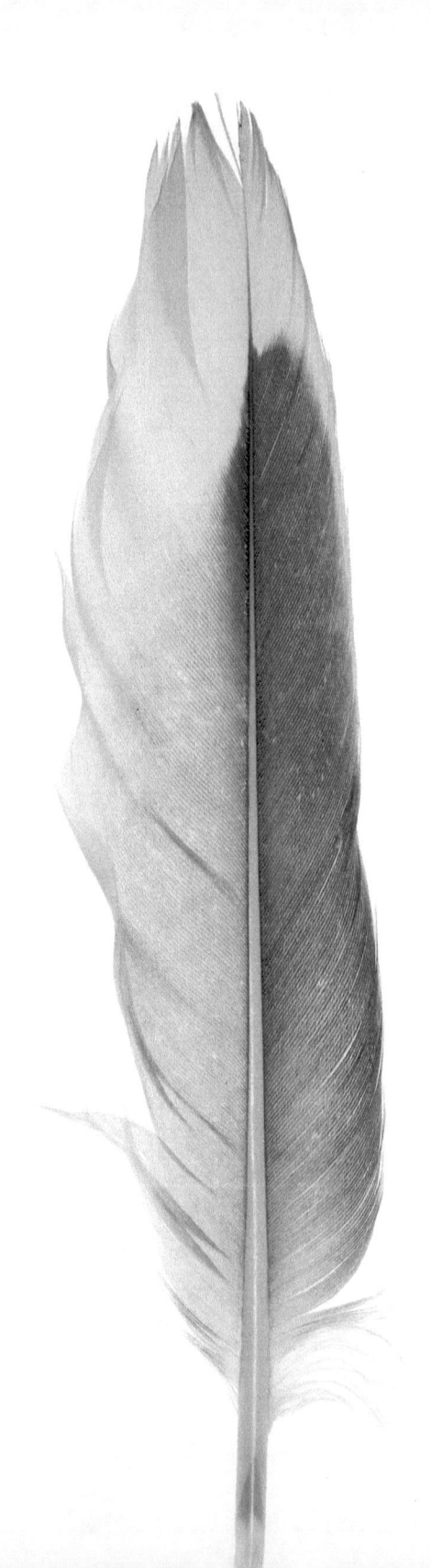

Flight feathers
POEMS

GWENDOLYN MORGAN

WAYFARER BOOKS
BERKSHIRE MOUNTAINS, MASS.

WWW.WAYFARERBOOKS.ORG

© 2022 TEXT BY GWENDOLYN MORGAN
All Rights Reserved
Published in 2022 by Wayfarer Books
An Imprint of Homebound Publications

Wayfarer Books supports copyright. Copyright fuels creativity, encourages diverse voices, promotes free speech, and creates a vibrant culture. Thank you for buying an authorized edition of this book and for complying with copyright laws by not reproducing, scanning, or distributing any part of it in any form without permission. You are supporting writers and allowing us to continue to publish books for every reader.

Due to the author's commitment to confidentiality the people and circumstances portrayed in these poems are composite in nature. Any person or circumstance represents a combination of many individuals and events from over two decades of service in interfaith spiritual care in various settings. Any resemblance of a composite to an actual person or event is coincidental.

Cover Design and Interior Design by Leslie M. Browning
Cover Image: © Susan Bourde, "Sky King's Castle,"
the watercolor of Peregrine Falcon.
Interior Feather Image: © DrPas
First Edition Trade Paperback 978-1-956368-12-3
Also Available in eBook.
10 9 8 7 6 5 4 3 2 1

in  Wayfarer Books is committed to ecological stewardship. We greatly value the natural environment and invest in environmental conservation. For each book purchased our online store we plant one tree.

ALSO BY THE AUTHOR

Crow Feathers, Red Ochre, Green Tea
Snowy Owls, Egrets, and Unexpected Graces
Before the Sun Rise

Contents

1   Heart, Zendo

FIELD NOTES

5   A Note to Spotted Towhee
6   She said the Moon is in Cancer, her home sign
8   She was once a rainforest
10   She (who) listens to botanicals
11   Botanical Key: Bud scale Scar
13   Flight Feathers
14   light, sound, bone
16   Culinary observations from an organic perspective
19   Gratitude Field Notes
20   Writing her way home
21   149 Mile Post
22   Autumnal Detention Center
23   Trauma-informed Care
24   Mourning, Soapstone Creek
25   It is morning
26   She (who) speaks river language
27   Salt, Fragments
28   Commitment
30   Incandescent
32   3-whorled light
33   She (who) gathers mushrooms

STENCILS: FLIGHT FEATHERS OF GRIEF & GRATITUDE

- 37 Stencil no. i: tonight I write the saddest lines
- 39 Stencil no. ii: Red Fox, ICU
- 41 Stencil no. iii: Grandmother's Stencils—
- 43 Stencil no iv: Egrets and Flamingos in Patagonia
- 45 Stencil no. v: Medicine Basket
- 46 Stencil no. vi: Chickaree & little animals in the woods

MIGRATIONS

- 53 Improvisation, Scaled Down, ICU
- 55 Western Bluebirds, American Robins
- 57 Penguin: Family Speniscidae
- 59 Raccoon, Lady Liberty
- 61 Migrations
- 63 Blend, coffee, clay
- 64 Salish Sea, Songs of Grief
- 66 how to name a constellation
- 68 The North Star
- 70 Leporidae, mixed media
- 72 Pisces Moon Sunrise, Rain
- 73 American Bittern

74 She (who) remembers Autumn
75 The cure for soul loss
76 Sandhill Cranes
77 Caminito, Via Dolorosa
78 Imbolc, Cassiopeia
80 what counts is your practice of hospitality
81 Postlude: White Ptarmigans

Acknowledgments
About the Author
About the Press

Heart, Zendo

Her heart alone cannot
bear the sorrow of the world.
Yes, she has tried this practice.

This morning she drinks tea
by the river, stirs in wild honey, milk,
gladness. Under the eaves

in her room
she listens to the song of the rain
until the meditation bell rings.

Gratitude enkindles light:
a grateful heart
illuminates the space around it.

Field Notes

A Note to Spotted Towhee

Listen, the clouds move slowly, sun-lit
black-tailed deer with wild bird seed on their noses
translate hoof prints, western red cedar,
and stories of opossum

perhaps an artist dips her horsehair brush
into a palette of fluorescent paint
salmon-pink, mandarin orange sunrise,
feathers the color of musical notes.

Listen, the deer stand with you, near the wild roses
What stories are you going to tell?

She said the Moon is in Cancer, her home sign

the eucalyptus leaves   silvery
the fry bread   the pita bread

the communion wafer   the tortilla
all lunar invocations   to be taken by mouth

the Pacific Wren takes the wings of an insect
diaphanous light   into its beak

dragonfly   house fly   flying ant
she said cancer cells reproduced like morning glory

she arranged flowers every morning
larkspur, wild cosmos, scarlet flax

she listened to lilies   roses   fern fronds   teasel
listened to bee wings   crickets   gathering of
winged ones

they told her how to arrange the flowers
the cells arranged themselves erratically

the oral chemo the oral wash
to take the metallic taste away

she unfurled the prayer cloth
prayer wings of swallow: cliff or violet-green

invocation of flying insects   biting mouth parts
grasshopper cricket   luna moth   voices

repetition of musical instruments
flower   petal   stamen

crickets file and scraper in its wings
many eyes   many cells

she crossed over
many moons ago.

She was once a rainforest

underpinned with understory
crowned with a dense canopy
the Golden-crowned Kinglets spoke to her
before the White-breasted Nuthatch returned

      chi-chi-chi   watch your chi
      kwi kwi kwi   they repeated

seven years in the wilderness
below the swollen lymph nodes
nodules   she thinks she can't breathe
when breath   wind   spirit

ruach πνεῦμα prana   qi   aliento
the same word in hundreds of languages
she has forgotten her language of rain
rain wind indweller

sky-holder and the humans remind her
tzzt   just let it hum in your throat

mi alma   azul turquoise   aquamarine
cerulean cierto cobalt   cyna skyway

hummingbird blue is the color of love she said
Steller's Jay said blue is the new black
cancer round in her belly in her throat in her thyroid
a tumor like a coelenterate   soft mucinous

she drinks in Pacific Yew trees
plants them around her yard taxol taxotere
moss green   forest green   healing green
the birds are speaking a language of understory

the ground shifts beneath her
earth heart beat rattle hum
it is raining somewhere.

She (who) Listens to Botanicals

She walks through a recent burn, wildfire
this year fire traveled fifty miles an hour

flames leaped over stretches, patches left unburned
torched wild grasses, wildflowers

firestorms left remnants of gray powder
ashes, organic material vaporized

Douglas Fir may mitigate climate change
like her, better without fire.

She studies brush lettering, line drawing
her botanicals in shapes of cuneiform

wedges, wishes, living wills
light yellow green, sap green inscriptions

lichens, mosses, ferns smoldering
with stories, edible thistle

herbaceous biennial, balsam root
strong starches, impressions

She listens to their ancestors
cellular manuscripts of her descendants.

Botanical Key: Bud Scale Scar

She takes a news Sabbath, then returns
to plein air painting, too many facist global scars
not just one year of climate change or pandemic.

She learns how government workers changed each database
undoing years of previous scientific research.

Robin's alarm, Steller's Jay
Where is Spotted Owl?

She listens to avian notes of Great Horned Owl
with ear tufts set wide apart
yellow eyes flecked with gold
mottled grey brown above
gilded like her memory.

She returns to study lenticels, pores on the surface
of each plant for breaking through stems
they occur in clumps like cancer
reproducing faster than healthy cells
faster than the rise of waters along the coast.

She learns of bud scale scar—one scar noting location
of last year's terminal bud.

In the morning she watches White-tailed Deer
walks among wild black cherry trees
pauses with dog-whistle alarm call of Robin
shook shook shook of jay
owl's flight in the canopy.

She returns to bud scales, terminal illness
warning, scars on the tree limbs, mining data
forcible suppression of opposition
cross bars on secondaries.
Don't say we are not all complicit.

Don't say the robin, the jay, the owl did not warn us
each morning with their light and song.

Flight Feathers

We found a large flight feather
watched Red-tailed Hawk on a thermal lift
when it started to rain, we remembered.

The mother told us they put an ankle bracelet
on her when they separated her
from her children at the border crossing.

This is the same bracelets our government
uses to track prisoners, electronic surveillance
a way to monitor movement of undocumented.

The mother shared that ICE
kept her two children in cages for months
"They treated us like animals,"

she wrote in her notebook,
"they confirmed my identity
with facial recognition."

We confirmed the identification of the hawk
with Feather Atlas, a field guide to feathers
from the Forensics Laboratory
of the U.S. Fish and Wildlife Service.

LIGHT, SOUND, BONE

Hermit Thrush, Swainson's Thrush
flutelike intricate inspirations
elaborations   embroidered embellishments
variations from established climate patterns

vibrations of notes, patterns, shiny shells, buttons
produced by the syrinx in the windpipe
peace pipe   grouse snipe
woodcock   nighthawk   everyone vocal

drumming of Acorn Woodpecker on hollow tree
she rises on thermals, prevailing winds from the west
from the ocean, over the Cascade Range
nothing feels the same, looks the same

Tundra Swan feathers   Snow Goose feathers
Golden Eagle feathers   Raven feathers
how the wind lifts the bones   the melodies
vibrations of light, sound, bone

how to be a hollow bone, naming birds, weather patterns
how to let the wind speak through her sorrow
how to protest the violence, environmental destruction
hurricane, tornado, tsunami

sound a gesture
a song   one found consonant
release adjective, adverb, torrential sorrow
sign another petition, stand in the rain of her precinct

unprecedented monsoon rains in the Pacific Northwest
she takes organic non-GMO heirloom seeds into her teeth
sends songs to Greta Thunberg, her grandchildren
immigrant children on the borderlands

blue songs   blue star niños
ultra-violet violet-blue
intrasolar   interlunar   interplanetary aura of
imaginary wings and memories

she bones her way across centuries of poverty, protest
carries melodies of what it means to care for the earth
dawning awareness
before the birds sing

before the first sign of light
she remembers how to be vocal.

Culinary Observations from an Organic Perspective

circles within circles, spirals of magenta,
orange, cadmium yellow

the red beet   the golden beet
kohlrabi   black radish

rainbow carrots   Peruvian purple potatoes
thick dinosaur kale   red chard

yellow pear tomatoes   heirloom tomatoes
seeds saved from her great aunt

Cascade Chinook, Watlala band
organics from another century

North Star Polaris Kale   garlic   sweet onion
burgundy garlic   privilege of garlic braids

she chops for hours, knife on wooden cutting board
knife to legume, greens, nightshade, root vegetables

her aunt is standing next to a dugout canoe
at the river's edge

black and white photo framed in a heavy wood

pencil drawings of pints & quarts
of pickled green beans and asparagus

watercolors of white and yellow peaches
that line the cedar pantry

garlic and fennel floating near the top of dill pickles
smaller jars of blackberry syrup,

raspberry jam, plum jelly
salmon, canned sockeye salmon in smaller canning jars

glass with diamonds like fish scales
thousands of salmon then, even in the smaller creeks

the women dried the salmon on wood
along the banks of the Wind River

a hundred acres of oak and ash,
cedar and fir   timber nearby

older than we are, they face
the climate fires we have created

the chickens from Kelley's Coop
are still talking in decades

scratching hieroglyphics in the garden near the rabbits
the hens climb up the wooden ladder to roost at night

not far from where the cedar canoes
 lay in the wild grasses

dandelion seeds clinging
 to sticky vines of remembrance

the Speckled Sussex hens, like us,
prefer their sweets early in the morning.

Gratitude Field Notes
1200 Beats Per Minute[1]

Gratitude enkindles light
Snow Geese
black wing tips
pink feet
wintering on
the British Columbian coast
the Gulf of Mexico
the Skagit Flats
near the 49th parallel.

She enters notes, sketches
Wandering Shrew
eat insects, larvae
arthropods, worms, conifer seeds
and underground-fruiting fungi
high caloric intake, extreme heart rate
1200 beats per minute
ferocious, solitary
each vole has complex
underground networks
entrances, burrows
tastes of succulent stem bases
root-crowns of grasses, wildflowers
lupine, valerian.

---

[1] The heart beat of a Wandering Shrew is 1200 beats per minute.

WRITING HER WAY HOME

Military jets overhead
more frequently now
textual footnotes warn about
social distance

cover your ears
hide under a desk
wear a mask
write a poem of protest

Call notes   etched in her memory
descending minors   insistent   obsessive
Titmice   repetitive rhythm
Black-capped Chickadees   repeated   *dee dee dee*
Golden-crowned Sparrows

She writes lyric poetry, buys postage stamps
waits for her turn at the post office desk
as a man in camouflage refuses to wear a mask
flinches at the sound of F-15 Eagle fighter jets.

149 Mile Post

Diminutive figure of the Snow Goose
the Ross Goose winters
in the San Joaquin Valley
in the spring it returns to the high north,
reappears again in her journal
over the same routes in autumn
white feathers, short pink bill, pink legs

Peace Arch Border customs
Border Point checkpoint
over 60 people of Iranian, Chinese, Mexican
descent, the vast majority of whom
are American Citizens like she, her, they, them
detained, questioned at length.

Peace be with you
Assalamu Alaikum.

Autumnal Detention Center

"ICE finds itself bedeviled
by activists, attorneys
and politicians in the Pacific Northwest
who are determined to gum up
the machines of immigrant enforcement."[2]

She remembers that a grateful heart
illuminates the space around it.

Underneath feathered clouds
she waits outside
the Immigration Detention Center.

With mothers from around the world
she leans against the cement wall
cries for her children.

Above rare "blue" (Snow Geese)
mostly dark bodies and wings
issue high-pitched laments.

---

[2] Richard Read, "The Northwest turns up the heat on ICE" *LAtimes.com*, ICE: Immigration and Customs Enforcement.

Trauma-informed Care

No estas sola
she is a resident of a state
"diametrically opposed to
the national policies of enforcement
resisting immigration practices
that are espousing
human rights violations."

She says they need to stop disorientation
stop separation of parents from children
as she keeps social distance

even geese know better
how to care for their young
a grateful heart illuminates

trauma-informed care
fluorescent lights overhead
she watches the seasonal migration

of birds, farm workers, retraumatization
repeat: "What do our
descendants ask of us?"

Mourning, Soapstone Creek

She let the words fall by a secluded wood
within, one who has not forgotten
the curve of water stanza
Wood Thrush, Varied Thrush, the names of trees
the language of old roots
forming hollows where fish hid
mosses, ancestors
morning rain, light on ink
and everywhere, the forest is shrouded,
fog, mist, cloud, smoke
a river winding round a solitary figure
remembers ten thousand things
brings to light, present tense.

It is Morning

Kindling
small sticks
round sticks
newspaper, crumpled
strike match and watch the paper turn
to flame. Feel the warmth, the light.
this is the only day you have to love
and be loved, to light and be light
she (who) will kindle love this morning
she (who) will make tea with honey, amber light
and whole goat's milk
black tea from India
she (who) will speak with compassion, metta
lovingkindness practice
she (who) will greet the wren, the kingfisher,
the deer, the squirrel, the red fox
The sun when it rises above the trees
she (who) will keep water warm in my tea kettle
she (who) will keep love warm in my heart
round sticks
small sticks
kindling.

She (Who) Speaks River Language

the vocation of water is fluidity
before she tells herself
where she will flow
she (who) is already on her way to the sea.
Listen! Song of Ouzel, rock-hewn gorge,
river-stone, White-tailed Deer, Wandering Shrew
petroglyph, alder, hemlock, fir
mossy banks and branches
smell of dinghy and kayak.

She memorizes the dialect of molecular structure,
and re-members the clay bottom, the subtext.
She never forgets who she is,
or where.

Salt, Fragments

This is the stalk of silver sea grass
the color of sky

snail
mussel
clam

shells broken
jagged

this is the water
how it is laden with salt.

She draws carefully in archival ink
adds water, color, highlights

listens to the call notes
etches in majors
descending minors
repeated intention

seeds
heart beats
wishes.

COMMITMENT

Peregrine Falcon sigils, steep angel of descent
glissando   spellcraft   Pacific seabird
30 degrees Fahrenheit   repetitive feather shafts

attentive to physical sensations
be responsible for making changes happen
keep focus   wings pointed

vestment   investment   commitment
dive with wings folded
guided by flight feathers

long-tailed ducks
dive deeper than many other ducks
like the falcon's momentum = velocity x mass

the slate blue wings catch our attention
dark brown airborne   white beneath
how the raptors rapt revel

raptores vocative plural
convergent evolution
rapid changes in flight direction

feel the physical sensation in your body when emotions arise
a long arc of knowing
a logarithmic cardiac spiral

examine what happens with curiosity
determine what your intention for the practice will be each morning.

Incandescent
Latitude 48.141578 Longitude -122.756939

She went for a walk
near the dangerous bluffs
overlooking the Salish Sea
6,503 miles from Al-Lādhiqīyah, Syria

She wants you to know
these bone fragments
these viruses, seed pods
limbs of green-blue fir
brown children's limbs, women's limbs

She could not remember the bombing
thousands of miles from Tehran and Hong Kong
the Peregrine Falcon sweeping seaward.

    ii

Incandescent the earth hums
the Columbian Black-tailed Deer chew the apples slowly
landscape on a cotton stretched canvas
the woman paints pastoral settings
olive orchards, flower gardens
sweetness of honey
the deer step carefully on the moss
ears forward, backward.

As she paints, she listens for bombs detonating
listens for viruses, bone fragments
immigration raids
manuscripts, colors
letters in Arabic, Chinese, Spanish
hoof prints.

3-WHORLED LIGHT

patterns of fern fronds, fragile fern, lady fern, wood fern
leaves of herbs, fused petals, she often names the leaves
one afternoon she can't seem to name anything
a blur of post-menopausal chemo plus COVID-19 detritus

then names return: dogbane leaves, leaves opposite, oval
icicle moss, big shaggy moss, colors and tastes, licorice and cinnamon
aspects of tree trunks, Aries Sun sextile to Saturn
star light coming into the middle canopy

moist barks, lichens, cambium stripped by a black bear
striped skunk, glossy black 2 white stripes diverging at the nape
run down the back, conspicuous, recognized
like syllables from the lost worlds, lost light

she is on a round of returns, declinations
like a long-tailed weasel foraging at first light
how to be light: celestial light
of 3-whorled juniper leaves

Pacific tree frogs finding homes
gophers create shelter for the chorus frogs
during a fire   we create patterns of connection
light in this industrial forest of isolation.

She (Who) Gathers Mushrooms

When the sun rose above
the cascade peaks
she laced her hiking boots, retraced
her steps like Raven following rain clouds
she knows the names of ink cap
blue chanterelle, black morel,
the understory
the forest floor
illuminates her path
to perceive the natural world
through traditional ways of being
elemental knowing   leaf detritus
the forest lessons of ash leaves, white fir needles
mouse-tail moss, lichens, new territory of rhizomes
she wishes the children in the shelter, in the cages
could taste the sweet licorice root
touch yellow-green mosses
place rings of bracken ferns around
small brown earth hands.

She walks into this territory underground
ancestral land   emergent layers, dense canopy
enormous mushroom shaped crowns
thousands of persons without homes now
she knows they will be wandering
seeking home for decades

if they survive   as she has survived so far
guessing the names of other plants
her grandmother pointed out the ones you could eat
the ones to avoid   immigration officers
skulking in the shadows   others waiting to evict
the wild ones, tented beneath Douglas Fir
her boots leave clear tracks
in the places where the latest news
dampens her hopes   as she remembers

light a candle of invocation
change consciousness
like a chalice of golden chanterelles.
may courage sustain us all.

Stencils
Flight Feathers of Grief & Gratitude

STENCIL NO. 1:
Tonight I write the saddest lines

Acorn Woodpecker, conspicuous amongst the deciduous trees, clownish "whecka whecka,"

this morning's nasal congestion, a complex family system. I feel sadness and the sorrow of the world. Distinctive red, black and white feathers of head pattern, the patterns of the oak bark, the replication of the coronavirus, our familial grief in the foreground, global grief in the background. Systemic pandemic, systemic racism, systemic poverty, ecological devastation, yet the bird song fills the morning around us, rising at first light, falling again after sunrise.

At Westerbeke Ranch at a training, four years and certain degrees of light ago, Acorn Woodpecker greeting me daily. Each morning, accelerating drumming mirrored my own cardiac drumming when my cell phone buzzed again. My father had had a series of strokes years before and it was becoming increasingly clear that his wife of twenty-five years was abandoning him to his adult children, and as the responsible daughter, the caregiving would rest on my shoulders. Distinctive patterns of abandonment, unreported elder abuse, and the legal system. Not uncommon for elders, like this bird before me.

Woodpeckers, sapsuckers, and allies. Chisel-billed, wood-boring beaks, full of winged insects, the stories I would learn of this family. Picidae. Stories I would learn of our family. Tonight I write the saddest lines with quill, black-shafted feathers. I didn't tell you my father died a few months ago just before his 84th birthday after four years of our and others' caregiving. In the middle of COVID-19 yet not Covid-related. We sat vigil bedside for two days and nights, watching the birds outside—towhee, robin, chickadee, sparrow, finch, crow. The Garry oak, walnut trees, and pine hemming in the adult family home. His friend's Native American Flute CD playing over and over, tone variations of various instruments. His Latinx caregiver singing to him *Papicíto, Papicíto*. The week before I sat with more than one family via iPad, their family members, fathers, brothers dying of COVID-19 and other health challenges. Each person was younger than my own father. White skin, brown skin, many voices, multi-lingual conversations in the patterns of the Zoom connection. Gallery view to show us gathered in gratitude and grief. Our interconnected multi-ethnic families: Black, white, red.

STENCIL NO. 11
Red Fox, ICU

The red fox trots past red bricks of the 7-story hospital into the green space of the Salmon Creek watershed. To the east, vendors set up the Farmer's Market booths in the contractor's parking lot: organic vegetables, berries and peaches, bouquets of flowers, lavender, wildflower honey, native plants, Middle Eastern cuisine and bagels. A physician hesitates before the berry farm booth, suspicious of the "no spray" blackberries. There is a dank smell of swamp from the creek like dead frogs, the dry season following fall equinox.

Three stories up there is an autumnal heaviness in the Intensive Care Unit. Three seasoned nurses in personal protective equipment, PPE—this time the full hazmat look—preparing to enter the same room again. Accustomed to the hypervigilance with this invisible virus and viruses flying haphazardly across the unit with an unexpected sneeze of a hospitalist who just walked through the doors. Another physician had stepped out into the healing garden to take a phone call from their family on another continent. Staff from around the world share they are anxious about their families. The fox turns, looks up, as if this canine can sense that someone is near death. Here, the anxiety, fatigue and sorrow of clinical staff is palpable. The art of medicine accompanied by the daily mantra acuity high, mortality high. The incessant beeping of monitors, IVs infiltrated, another patient going into acute crisis of respiratory failure. Here the administration of vasopressors is required to maintain a mean arterial pressure: (MAP).   One of the hospitalists has topographic maps of Pacific Northwest trails strewn in the back of their truck, hiking boots with dried mud, a stainless-steel water bottle with "Defenders of Wildlife" wolves etched on the cylinder. They are acutely aware they are on day 3 of a 7-day stint.   Spiritual distress smells like sepsis. Yet at night you can see Sirius the Dog Star, First Quarter of the Moon.

Outside a series of Northwestern Crows repeat the stories in Corvidae lines.   An RN checks the placement of a peripheral intravenous line, squeezes a sachet of lavender in their pocket. One of the techs bought everyone lavender at the farmers market, organic French lavender. Lavender and coffee grounds now rest on the bedside table to erase the memory of loss and feces. The memory of how many persons have died in this room alone.   The contrast of loose stool, the smell of coffee, bleach, and lavender. Respiratory failure.   Exhaustion. And then there is another call for report from the Emergency Department. They need an ICU bed and a language interpreter. The nurse sighs as the Crow flies toward the green space, above the fox, whose paws are black, dry as the banks of the creek, her throat. The Music Thanatologist arrives and sets her Celtic harp outside the room and begins to play.

STENCIL NO. III
Grandmother's Stencils—
Coniferous Forests, Wood Thrush

She wakes at first light, listens for the fluting song of the thrush
she slowly opens her eyes, reaches for distinctive spectacles
certain colors and memories lost in blackberry thickets
Swainson's Thrush in the sap green of alder, fir, and bramble
a lyrical stenciling of birdsong, familial remembrance
feathers spotted brown, the color of a hazelnut latte
then heaviness of dementia, vascular, the cambium
of my grandmother, my father's mother
who taught me the names of plants, birds, and flowers
Sword Fern, Bracken Fern, Deer Fern
American Robin, Varied Thrush, Hermit Thrush
Family of Thrushes and Thrashers
before she lost all memory of family names
her studio drawings, yellowed tracing paper
wood blocks, ceramics, and stencils
this contour of forgetting
this wisdom of grief
then, gratitude of wood sorrel and salal
the sweet taste of the licorice fern root
pulled from green gold mosses
she spent more time listening, lost
to her own sorrow gathered
walking in the woods naming flowers
purple slip of lady's slipper

furry of lamb's tongue
the slurred russet-backed poem of this thrush
this much I know: we ate chocolate from Switzerland and Costa Rica
she taught me how to hold still, how to listen in the woods
how to look for flight patterns of birds,
varicose veins, memories.

STENCIL NO IV
Egrets and Flamingos in Patagonia

There were egrets in Patagonia too. I fell in love with Lapwings and Flamingos. This was a childhood dream—to go to Punta Arenas and the furthermost tip of South America. El Fin del Mundo, Tierra del Fuego. It is a stretch of sea and sky like the tundra near St. Mary's, Alaska. The high desert of New Mexico where my maternal grandmother and her brothers lived. Taos. Abiquiú. Tesuque. Fishing villages in Alaska, Nova Scotia, Newfoundland, Chile, places I thought I might land like the Great Egret landing in front of me. Voice very deep like the Anishinaabe Elder who tells us that seeing a white bird was a good sign, good medicine. "Today is a good day to be born," they said. "Today is a good day to go home."

The Great Egret has a deep neck bow that adds to its elegance. As if the yellow bill and long neck would bring us unexpected treasures. I note how it waits like the herons, waiting to spear a fish or a frog. Family Ardeidae. It wades slowly in the creek, waiting. I too am waiting in this time of post-everything, listening carefully to conversations, the unconscious actions of others. The sound of my pen on the journal, quill scratching on paper made of certified cellulose pulp issued from forests managed according to strict environmental standards. Acid free. The oncologist tells the young woman to not wait to take a trip, previously suggested a cruise before cruises were lethal. Gently suggests to her to do those things that had been set aside yet were on her wish list. She looks up at me, asks: "Where would you like to go?"   She is nearing another stage in her treatment yet in a time of relative stability. She is wearing a pink top with flamingos.   Meditating daily, eating organic foods, in a place of clarity like the bitterns, herons and allies wading in marshes, creek beds, tidal flats. She starts to cry, reaches up, and takes our hands. Today is a good day to go home.

STENCIL NO. V
Medicine Basket

Gifted with a traditional woven cedar basket. Cedar woven, hand dyed with violet wood sorrel, purple flowers with yellow centers, encircled with Indian Blanket red flowers, yellow centers. The center of flower carpels, her hands, her familial metacarpals. She carries her father's stories, flute playing, notes of sadness. Stories with an oyster shell from Vashon Island, perhaps the last flute circle he attended, white sage from Montana, braided sweetgrass, lavender, salt, grandmother's tobacco. A Golden Eagle feather beaded with the Four Directions: Yellow, Red, Black, White. She adds a bear claw, also a gift, rose quartz healing heart, a Zuni bear fetish.
When someone dies, carry their ancestral gifts in a basket to the next constellations. Healing oneself, herself, healing the planet. Circles of petals, self-compassion, wild roses, star light. How she carries the medicinal plants, poetic forms, horsehair paint brushes to her descendants. She leaves the many griefs, addictions, blood betrayals, this generational sorrow in the stone circle outside the basket, outside the circle of cedar trees. Women's Medicine Basket, Oyster shell, Eagle Flight feather.

White Sage, sweetgrass, salt
salt water will wash the pain
 softly to the sea

STENCIL NO. VI
Chickaree & Little Animals in the Woods

(after another week working in a medical center in the seventh month of the pandemic)

Look for: Chickaree
            Masked Shrew
            Water Shrew
            Yellow-pine Chipmunk
            Heather Vole
            Western Jumping Mouse

The Douglas Squirrel or Chickaree runs across our cedar deck, looks like a Red Squirrel yet has dusky olive on the back, yellow-gold underneath. Both squirrels have much of the same lifestyle, not unlike us. A tree-hole nest, a tree house, a round needle-twig-bark nest lined inside with cedar bark and moss.

I sit at my writing desk which looks out at the cedar trees from the second story, cloistered from the world today and still in tears. Yesterday our team was offering bereavement support with the adult child of a parent who died, and another and another. Thursday just around midnight our on-call chaplain attended four deaths in nearly one hour. "They went together," the nurse said the next morning. A Little Brown Creeper notches up the western red cedar in front of me followed by a White-breasted Nuthatch.

Saturday at the grocery store, I almost have a melt down between the organic almond milk and cashew yogurt selections. I watch the tall young muscled white man not wearing his mask brush past an elderly woman for the fourth time. I had already asked the produce manager how they would address him. The other stockers and checkers looked stricken. The young woman with him, wearing a mask and carrying a wicker basket, looked like the deer in front of our house when they hear a gunshot. From my work at the hospital, I knew not to confront him, and when my spouse began, "Sir!" I grabbed her—my white hands on her black arms—surprising myself, face to face, "Let them address him."

"Well, they're not," she said. Microaggression upon microaggression, trauma upon trauma triggering both of us.

"Honey, I have seen too many people erupt into violence. Please let them address it…" thinking he's probably packing a gun and would not flinch or even twitch when he shot someone in the face, "Let him go."

I turn to the clerk who is frozen by the yogurt shelves, "I saw someone die again yesterday. It's not a joke." The young man continues walking up and down the aisles, touching things randomly, arrogantly. I try to have compassion not knowing what his lack of cognitive awareness resulted from given his life history (assessment: Adverse Child Events indicate high ACE scores, drugs, politics, or sheer macho bravado). Yet I heard my voice rising to a higher pitch. I was going to be that hysterical middle-aged woman in the grocery story. I put spinach tortillas in our cart. Yellow peaches. Sweet Walla Walla onions. Most of our organic produce comes from the local farms. Tilth certified organic. Privilege of what we purchase, what we say, what we give, what we receive. Two young black men have been shot by police less than a mile from the grocery store. Shot dead.

The hand sewn comfort quilts we give to the grieving families are works of art. Community gifts in innumerable quilt patterns— Friendship, Nine Patch, Pinwheel, Rose of Sharon, Eight-pointed Star, Crazy Quilt. A color wheel of stars, squares, circles, spirals in a vast color palette. Today earthen brown, turquoise, ochre, lemon, and lavender. Wildflowers, roses, pansies, wolves, teacups, and cats, each adorned with a symbol for someone. Each given to someone who is nearing the end of life, or their loved ones following a death.

If the person died from COVID-19, we often meet the family in the main lobby, in front of the screening station where staff take the temperatures of staff and visitors, quickly assess their health, and give them a mask. Usually a spouse, an adult child, or a friend will pick up the quilt, quickly along with a bereavement packet. Occasionally a security officer will meet us with the person's belongings. Later the bereaved family may tell us they unfold the quilt in their living room and cry, noting the patchwork of colors, remembering their beloved. How suddenly they became ill, how quickly they died. The squirrels race across their back decks too, carrying seeds and nuts to bury in the ground, like grief, to be tended later. The Chickaree turns and looks at me, chattering about its cache of Douglas Fir cones. We haven't seen the red fox in the buffer zone of green space at the hospital in months.

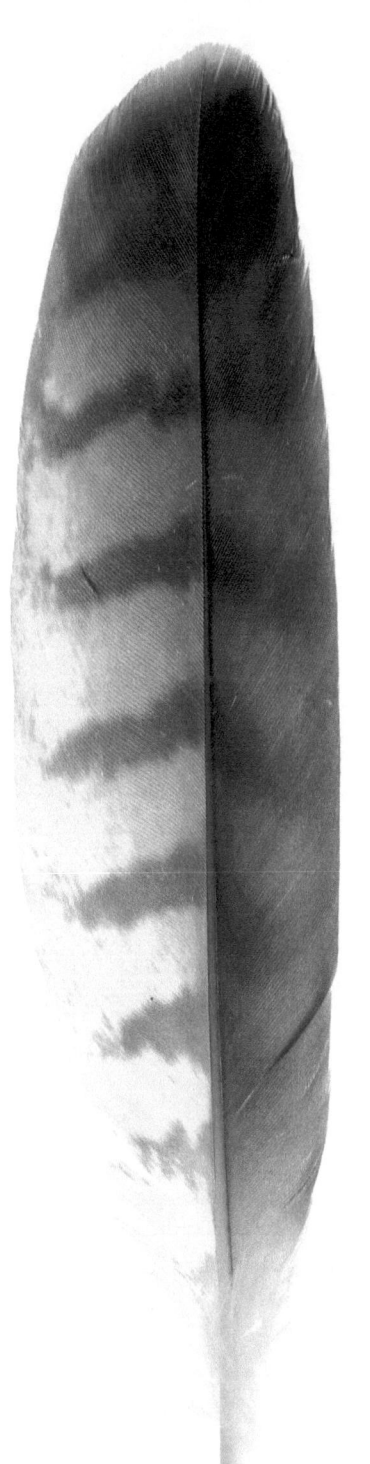

Migrations

Improvisation, Scaled Down, ICU

"It's enough that you are in the world."
–Idea Vilariño, Uruguayan poet (1920-2009)

We watched someone die of COVID-19
yesterday dying   mix and riff
of dysfunctional and functional familial grief
in the Intensive Care Unit

She watches the crows, American Crows, take a bath
in the round whole note
of the ceramic bird bath

We watched someone's mother,
father, dying of the Coronavirus disease
the day before   we are holding our breath

Then Robins, American Robins, follow, next in line
the next stanza of bird bath
then the little birds   quarter notes repeated

Then a young man with young children
he wasn't ready to pick up the improv
of pandemic   virus   death   prolonged grief
a ballad no, a requiem
not jazz not today
only the Steller's Jays ratcheting up the mix

Someone in Uruguay is drinking *un cafécito*
reading *Idea Vilariño*
es suficiente que estas en el mundo
it is enough that you are in the world

each day, they eat pink pan dulce, sweet bread
there is a sparrow eating breadcrumbs under the table
each day the birds remind me who I am.

Western Bluebirds, American Robins at the Peace & Justice (virtual) Fair
(Vancouver, U.S.A.)

this is how it begins
first light: cheerio song of Robins
loops of blue sky between stars
Eagle whistles before anyone wakes up
prayers in Arabic, Spanish, Hebrew
Chuukese, Cambodian, Russian, Swahili
100 languages spoken here as
the alphabet arcs toward aleph
alleluia of red-breasted Robins
golden dome of Sikh temple
Celtic Cross of Catholic, Presbyterian & Unity Church
Methodist or Lutheran hymns, so many Christians
the Bahá'ís and UUs have every symbol represented
even the Pagans are putting peanut butter & raspberry jam
on whole wheat toast before you
Who is putting honey on sopapillas, honeycrisp apples,
drinking Masala chai or sweet tea?
looking at privilege:
Who was evicted this week?
Who was arrested?
Break it down like the U.S. census
the unmarked car outside the housing complex
"No solicitors" sign outside the apartment door
"I'm not soliciting" the ICE agent says
flashes a silver star or gold badge with implicit bias

scan the skin color, then license plate
drinking an Americano while they wait for you
Wait! this isn't justice
the peace & justice fair is on Saturday every year
Sabbath day of rest for everyone
who goes to a synagogue or is Seventh Day
Rainbow Flags flying next to Black Lives Matter
upside down Americana
the Western Bluebirds gather at the river
singing their own prayers, plain song
1000 languages, songs of other species, intersectionality
the watershed of white fragility, white supremacy
unspoken privilege of having more than enough
when the child in front of you hasn't had breakfast
no money in the purse for groceries, no savings account
no internet access, maybe a chrome book from school
with a sticker of a white llama on it
this child is hungry for more than justice
losing their breath for peace
this is how it begins.

Penguin: Family Spheniscidae

aquatic flightless birds
like us   have adapted to their environment
adopted flippers for swimming in icy water
in Chile, Argentina, South Africa

We are a black and white same gendered
multiracial family
intersectionality of lens
lock and intersect
race   ethnicity
gender   orientation
privilege   power
white and black witness feathers

our neighbor a white man swerved at us intentionally
gunned his engine again
a sandy brown vehicle
like the burnt umber sand at the edge of Ushuaia
where you can take a boat
to see three species of penguins
his Toyota 4Runner once and another black SUV again

revved at us   make the black woman
jump   again
and her partner jump
to our neighbor's green and brown grass

the couple moved here from another state
moved here a few years ago
now still shocked by the behavior
of well-educated privileged mostly white neighbors
who pack guns, rev engines, use anti-kind vernacular

watch microaggression after macroaggression
directed at my beloved   like guns, tear gas
and a palette of vehicles
rainbow of colors
the neighborhood children walk here too

I could write for days
about what it means to live here in black and white
how we have plush penguins
and carved wooden penguins
on our fireplace hearth
along with sage, sweetgrass, feathers,
ashes, vigil candles, gifts from our elders.

Raccoon, Lady Liberty

Procyon lotor

First light, gray with a soft black mask across her eyes
Mama Raccoon cries out, thick-set, brushy-furred
warning vocalizations we have never heard before.

Stars overhead, thin line of light on the eastern horizon
she hovers over her two babies,
crying out over and over.

The sound is close to the time
her neighbors trapped a baby raccoon.
Mama Raccoon ran up and down her yard

near the boundary line
crying and crying. She begged the family to release the baby
from the cage:

we live near a wildlife sanctuary,
of course, we are going to have raccoons.

Now she writes letters asking ICE to release babies
children from cages and detention centers, children wailing while
their Mamas' crying sound

carries across our nation.
Mamas wearing masks, gray with smoke and ash amidst the
pandemics.

We live near to one of two borders,
of course, we are a sanctuary of welcome

for the tired, the poor, the weary of the world yearning
to breathe free.[3]

Mama Raccoon picks up one baby by the scruff
carries it to shelter

the other little one follows her into the rose hips, ferns,
and cedar trees.

---

[3] ICE: Immigration and Customs Enforcement. Emma Lazarus, "The New Colossus," November 2, 1883. "Give me your tired, your poor, Your huddled masses yearning to breathe free, The wretched refuse of your teeming shore. Send these, the homeless, tempest-tossed to me, I lift my lamp beside the golden door!" The Statue of Liberty-Ellis Island Foundation, Inc.

Migrations

"Have you noticed all the birds?" she asked
pen poised on paper
a dancer, everything en pointe
she could pirouette as a little girl
the world around her on point
now the political plié
at the barre, a Supreme Court turn-out

she said she was seeing more birds than ever
in the midst of this pandemic
her handwriting suffered, shed curves rather than virus
she wrote in broken italic letters, missed cues
the r's blending into the s's
dots of i's and crooked t's
yet she danced chiaroscuro every day

dozens of Cedar Waxwings fill the hawthorn trees
reflected by dozens of Robins
a pair of Red-shafted Flickers, Varied Thrush
they pecked at small insects between
mini clover seeds, wild grasses
her emotions the cast shadow
a flutter of feathers like tutus

Black-capped Chickadee then California Scrub-Jays
take turns, gather one sunflower seed at a time
Mourning Doves beneath the feeders
her anxiety flits above them in the trees

yes, this is how her/their day started
with birds: passerines, waterfowl
even owls before the sun rose

storm clouds on the northwestern horizon,
across the river accusations of alt right
democratic governors compared to Hitler

Nazi flags flying behind the elected representative
Washington State, then Michigan militia choreography
partisan racial gerrymandering, map by map
she could barely listen, take notes, field sketches
in a time of irresponsible fascism.

Have you noticed all the birds?

Blend, Coffee, Clay

Brimmed coffee cup
teal flowers on clay
the coffee beans come from Guatemala
red poinsettias bloom on other holidays
white salt on white of egg, white of eye
she tries to find her way
out of glaucoma, macular degeneration
loss of vision and determination
metastatic cancer, bone metastases blocking reason
COVID-19 detritus, crows outside the hospital
she chooses a feeding tube, a j-peg
not an image from a photograph
yet a circular loop of plastic
that takes white artificial nutrition directly
to the stomach, axis mundi
center of the thought, the flower

how does she begin to hold
the cup in her trembling hands?

Salish Sea, Songs of Grief

She sits bedside, listens to breath
tastes the salt water   alone
blue-gray   calm of sea
a blend of watercolors, tears
spectrum blue #32
mineral green #45.

The Common Mergansers surface and dive
long bills with a hooked tip
serrated edges for little fish catches
aquamarine, iridescent salt water
her father dying
friends dead
the world not so calm.

She creates new sculptures
from found objects, stories of
teasel, devil's claw, kelp, and lichen
alder cones become creatures
or crow goddesses
those who journey in the afterlife.

She watches the mergansers
slight crest, red bill, white throat
dive and surface
surface and dive
singing fish songs
songs of traveling.

She sings softly under her breath
undulation of wave
sea spray of sorrow and song
gathering roots, dried wood
family stories, beadwork
remembrances

this is how she keeps ancestors alive
burning tallow, seal oil in her lamp at night.

HOW TO NAME A FAMILY CONSTELLATION

She notes that the nine parts
of DNA have their counterparts
in the nine planets, their descendants

fever 102.7, ragged breath, palliative care
24-7 advanced care planning
turned into hospital, hospice vigils

how tealight   soul light   his telescope
from days of astronomy light of her black onyx eyes
the sea blue, cornflower blue, aquamarine

amethyst, lapis lazuli his favorite gemstones
when she loved fire opals
decade upon decade of naming stars and stones

the twenty-seven groups
of nucleic acid found in the cell, nebula
correspond to constellations, celestials

she traces the family tree from Alberta
to British Columbia, circles of islands
around the Salish Sea

hibiscus and lemongrass, Andromeda
black currant and cloudberry, star jasmine
how she remembers to taste the blossoms

days of vigil, one vigil after another
their deaths reposed like spores
viruses, surgical masks and breathing treatments

she draws sword fern, bracken fern
salal, foxglove, lupine, pen and ink, watercolor
Vishad, ley lines of sadness and deep sorrow

one round agate, a worn prayer bead, calcite
at dawn the sky tastes like wild roses, rose quartz
when she can taste again
dried flowers in her field guide, gemstones in her medicine pouch

how she walks in the shadows of their memories
Anna's hummingbird, Townsend's chipmunk
Evening Grosbeak flies past ten thousand years

Swadharma, "the indwelling light" galactic Lascaux
yajña indicates mutual dependence, interdependence
how the entire universe is connected in stories

she smells the sulphur of hot mineral springs of their childhood
celestial spheres of familial moonstone, star patterns
Sirius, Ursa Major, Pegasus, the Galatic Center

the brightest star, North Star, Pole Star
nominative, genitive, trientalis borealis
how she remembers Grandmother Moon, Father Sky.

The North Star

The crows gather here to listen to our poems
they too recite poems, discuss Corvidae politics
poetics of black, gloss, shiny, flight feathers
green-gold moss grows slowly on red bricks

The crows eat the stars, our chocolate-covered shortbread cookies
chocolate brown stars embedded with white polestar sprinkles;
when we are not looking, they toss the stars over their shoulders
galactic cookies transform into celestials

the stars seen outside of Gallup, New Mexico
where little Maria de las Estrellas is counting galaxies
in the Milky Way from her adobe home.
She, like the crows, has not forgotten.

She has not forgotten the detention centers, the dog cages
otras niñas, other girls, other children like her sisters
waiting a few hundred miles away
dreaming of red, white, and blue cowboy boots

with the star-spangled banner stitched into the seams
black musical notations of equity and freedom.

Last week her sister wet her fuchsia pink sweatpants
in front of the ICE police agent, brown uniform with a silver star.

Her sadness turned into a poem,
a shiny star picked up by the crow

who flew through the rainstorm
through the sorrow and protests
following the North Star here
to the center of the world to remind us:

Por favor,
do not forget your children.

Leporidae, Mixed Media
Oryctolagus Cuniculus

The European rabbit painting
involves the use of 2 or more artistic medium

eclectic combination of her grandmother's
buttons, acrylic paints, mixed primary colors

vintage beads, story lines, letters of the alphabet
small mammal teeth (primarily Rodentia)

Spanish words, detailed, intricate, an invitation to beauty
amid sorrow and daily dose of violence, mixed crowd

shooting in every city, the children too, the garlic festival
cloves of garlic praised as the elixir for all healing, mixta

peel the layers of two, three years of plantings, paintings
plantations mined with toxic chemicals, lies, buried

dyed orange hair, racist xenophobic misogynist policies
more than one media utilized to disseminate hate not beauty

alternative views of the universe
domesticated coney, or wild with long ears, short tails

they used 2 forms of chemotherapy for her treatment
mixed media: Taxol (Pacific Yew) and cisplatin

heavy metal, a deep yellow-orange crystalline powder
plus cloves of garlic, other herbal medicinals, acupuncture

and beliefs, her pink rabbit foot on the key chain,
her chakana from Peru
a turquoise rosary blessed in St. Francis, Italy

the wild rabbit waits by the sword ferns
for her to bring organic carrots at sunrise.

Pisces Moon Sunrise, Rain

Frogs announced the rain last night
gone are the airy frivolities of mid-summer
the heat packs the grasses dry
she is back in COVID-19 crisis again
the unnecessary mud and leaves
tracked on the clean kitchen floor
Mercury's trine to Chiron
and she can't help but talk
about her vulnerabilities: violets,
lavender, mullein, primrose
the yellow-green of frog
all her italic letters are written
with one stroke, one or two
she can't write now
or sign the informed consent document
X marks the spot where
she will begin her life.

AMERICAN BITTERN
BOTAURUS LENTIGINOSUS

Heavy-bodied, brown, secretive
the color of Peruvian light-roast
cadmium yellow bill, tapered neck with bold stripes
a deep repeated song, cinnamon brown

more nasal in flight, it flies over the algae-covered marsh
the weedy lake with trees smoldering from wildfires
she moves slowly through her thoughts
like the bittern, at times with rapid wing beat

rapid heartbeat, bitterness of politics
after the equinox the nights will grow longer
the wheel of the year turns past Mabon
like the waterwheel, spilling water over wood

this season it is a time to find more
balance in her life, Libra Sun. Libra Moon
in the midst of political firestorms, upheaval
of autumnal earth, landscape, hope

wildfires a bleak smell of burnt wood of sorrow
Mercury moves into the shadow zone
of the next retrograde before the election
the last of the apples and pears cling to branches

waiting to fall to the serpentine earth
bees gather around the bruised fruit
she watches the sky
waits for rain.

She (who) remembers Autumn

i's dotted with Ibis and Iceland Gull
t's crossed with Treecreeper and Tawny Owl
she says to notice this turning of the planet
the wheel of the year, Mabon to Samhain
thickening rain clouds like blackberry pie filling
nimbostratus rain clouds, cumulonimbus
clumps of thunder heads on the hills above
streaks of lightning, fires in the forest
nothing is black and white, she says
open the anthology of bird tracks
study strata, bones, sugar content
eight planets in retrograde
autumnal migration
immigrants, refugees in unsafe shelters
food shortages, food solidarity
her shoulders ache from bending
over her work in the world
the scapula, bones where the wings used to be
her memories briefly sketched in graphite and fatigue
appear as distance, absence, sorrow, fire
she gathers root vegetables, leaves of weeds
excerpts and line drawings of contour feathers, birds

she says *be open to receive*
messages from the universe.

The Cure for Soul Loss

Red-breasted Nuthatch re-mends the cosmos
calls three times
She calls on guardian spirits
of this place she calls home

three times within this intimacy of breath
the wind blew interior feathers
while geese circle
over Cougar Creek

she cut maples and cedars
round green prayer sticks
the trees remember their names
in the centrifugal ring of story

in order for her to heal
the natural world
must be taken
inside her body

listen, Nuthatch,
oh, little one, you carry
songs to the cedars
whistle at night

the constellations of Chickadee
and Saw-whet Owl cosmos
offer star stories, winged messengers
to heal the heart of the world.

Sandhill Cranes

Sandhill Cranes return
red crest, autumnal markers
before the turning of the wheel of the year
the solace of crane song
the pirouette of leg and bill

how they survive year after year
fields turned into housing complexes
marshes drained, flight patterns
disrupted by wildfires
yet somehow we hear them overhead
reminding us this life is possible.

Caminito, Via Dolorosa

There, by the western red cedar
the incandescent trail of a banana slug
then a garden snail, spirals of shell, memories
Heliotrope with large cordate leaves

Spotted Towhee, Collared Dove
eat seeds and small insects
now, along the deer path
the black-tailed doe and her twin fawns

step cautiously past sword fern
the salt lick on rain-moist clay
leaving small imprints of hooves
these too appear heart-shaped

it has been days since their last visit
she watches them meander through her yard
past the trellis of roses
and her heart wanders with them.

Imbolc, Cassiopeia

gratitude enkindles light
a grateful heart
illuminates the space
around it

a deer
may be described
by hoof and muzzle
a river by the sky
snowdrops on Candlemas

thankfulness
rises like a Tundra Swan
someone starts to hum
and the river
is the descant

the deer
come to the river
to drink each morning
watch
white-tailed deer enter sky
water refracts gratitude
as she drinks deeply

the sky grows light
with a swath of pale silk blue
between branches of myrtlewood
clusters of windflowers
and it could be
water, or Brigit
walking over her hearth
of dawn, singing,
illuminated.

WHAT COUNTS IS
YOUR PRACTICE OF HOSPITALITY

6x8 inches, cold press finish
pen & ink first, then watercolor wash
squares of black around the edges
a cup of sweet hot tea in Istanbul
chocolate caliente and churros in Mexico City
tea with milk and honey in Minneapolis
small bare feet on a hand-woven Persian rug
burnt red, gold, oat-colored fringes
a postcard arrives in the mail from Tijuana
a message from the borderlands
dearest Calliope, beautiful little star
we have not forgotten you.

White Ptarmigans

      She dreams
of
white
ptarmigans

against an azul sky
bird tracks   cloudlets
cryptic plumage

aurora borealis
pink rose quartz feet
high-pitched call

sadness
then
gratitude

      first light
of
morning

Acknowledgments

With gratitude to L.M. Browning, editor and publisher of Homebound Publications and Wayfarer Books, for flight feathers of encouragement, support and literary guidance. Thank you to the following publications and organizations in which these poems have previously been honored or printed, sometimes in slightly different forms.

Defending Home: anthology ed. by Ellen Waterston, August 2020: "Stencils: Flight Feathers of Grief and Gratitude"

Eco-Theo Review, Summer Issue 2020: "She said the Moon is in Cancer, her home sign"

Eco-Theo Review Summer Solstice online, https://www.ecotheo.org/two-poems-by-gwendolyn-morgan/: "A Note to Spotted Towhee"; "She was once a rainforest"

Moss, Volume Six, Autumn 2021: "Blend, clay, coffee"

Peace & Justice Fair: "Western Bluebirds, American Robins at the P&J 2020 (virtual) Fair (Vancouver, U.S.A.)"; The New Verse News, September 16, 2020 https://newversenews.blogspot.com/2020/09/western-bluebirds-american-robins.html

The Wayfarer: Autumn 2020: "Culinary Observations from an organic perspective"

The Wayfarer: Autumn 2021: "She (who) listens to bontanicals" "She (who) remembers Autumn."

Tiger Moth Review, Winter 2021: "She (who) gathers mushrooms"

New Verse News, July 8, 2020 https://newversenews.blogspot.com/: "Penguin: Family Spheniscidae"

Willamette Writers Summer Conference: "Improvisation, Scaled Down, ICU"

Writer's Digest: "The North Star" (honorable mention, 2020, poetry)

> *"...to carry grief in one hand and gratitude*
> *in the other and be stretched large by them."*
>
> –Francis Weller

Feathers have become a metaphor for me for all that lifts us up in the world. And flight feathers are a metaphor of those taking flight. Many whom have mentored me, and many I have accompanied, have taught me how we may live fully and die fully with beauty, upheld by wings

With gratitude to my beloved Judy A. Rose, Naomi Isabella, our friends and family… In memory of my father Robley King Morgan, and my maternal grandmothers Ina King Morgan and Meryl Gwendolyn McCallum.

With honor to all the thousands of people living with cancer and autoimmune disorders linked to environmental toxins, in memory of all those who have died of complications of COVID-19, poverty, violence and pandemics of racism and xenophobia. May we support all those who are living with long-term effects of trauma and illness and those who have cared for them. With thanks to the earth for holding our pain. Namaste to many artists, dreamers, musicians, poets and writers who are holding up the light of their artistic gifts for the healing of the planet.

Mil gracias a Claudia Castro Luna, Washington State Poet Laureate 2018-2021 for including our poetry community in her One River, Many Voices statewide project which dovetailed with my service as Clark County Poet Laureate 2018-2020. *También les agradezco un montóna para un communidad por poemas para la cuarentena.*

With much appreciation to Centrum for a Centrum Artists Residency in Winter 2020. A special thanks to Ellen Waterston for A Writing Ranch, and her virtual "Stencils" workshop at Summer Fishtrap 2020, and for writing companions in Defending Home. And much gratitude to Frank X. Walker and Summer Fishtrap writing companions 2021.

Much gratitude to Artist Trust, Humanities Washington, Arts Commission of Washington, Willamette Writers, Artstra and Clark County Arts Commission for supporting me and my family during my service as Clark County Poet Laureate. Continued thanksgiving for Michael Lerner, Francis Weller and Commonweal staff for Healing Circles and spaces. Thanks to Stephanie Austin, Rose Marcus. Typewriter Tarot (Claire Bowman and Cecily Sailer) and Leah Whitehorse for gifting us with wisdom of astrologic insights every lunar cycle. Appreciation to the Academy of American Poets, AWP, John Fox and the Institute for Poetic Medicine, PEN America, Poets and Writers, Sitka Center for Art and Ecology, and all arts organization working for equity and inclusion, peace and justice. Thank you to Vintage Books, an independent community bookstore. With gratitude to all the kindred spirits of Apifera Farm, Blackbird Ranch Farm Sanctuary, Lavender Dreams Farm and Donkey Rescue, Odd Man Inn, Defenders of Wildlife, Center for Biological Diversity, World Wildlife and all other animal care, environmental care, animal rescue organizations. In honor of Coyote Ridge Ranch, Danielle's organic honey, Kelley's Coop and Full Plate Farm, organic farms in the Southwest Washington Columbia River watershed. Many thanks to innumerable colleagues, compañeras, and friends of Salmon Creek.

With gratitude for all the guidance I received with editing and revisions, with special thanks to Virginia Konchan. Many thanks to Annie Finch, Yasodha Gopal, Ruby Hansen Murray, and Octavio Quintanilla for encouragement and support.

With gratitude to all my writing companions, teachers and mentors from earlier days in Sitka, Alaska; Sundance, Wyoming and the Pacific Northwest including Mrs. Aragon, Fred Bigjim, Debby Saito, Nancy Ricketts, Gaydell Collier and the Bear Lodge Writers. Gratitude to Sonali Sangeeta Balajee, Peter Boehlke, Margaret Hartsook, Patricia Pearce and Kip Leitner, Victoria Stein, Dawn Thompson and Karen Wood for holding creative space over the years. Muchas gracias a Lorena Caberello por cuidarme, mi papicito y nuestra familia.

This book was written among all the spirits of the Columbia River watershed, emerged with the light and loving-kindness of our larger community as well as the support of all our ancestors, angels, helping spirits and guides. May we all shelter in poems and feathers.

Special thanks to Susan Bourdet for the gift of "Sky King's Castle," the watercolor of Peregrine Falcon gracing the cover of this book.

About the Author

Gwendolyn Morgan is a Pacific Northwest poet and artist who has served in interfaith spiritual care in medical centers for nearly two decades. She learned the names of birds and inherited horsehair paint brushes and wooden paint boxes from her grandmothers. She is a recipient of a few residencies including a Centrum Artist Residency. The Clark County Poet Laureate 2018-2020 in Washington State, her third book of poetry, Before the Sun Rises is a Nautilus Silver Winner in Poetry. As a multiracial family in a multi-species watershed, they are committed to equity work and inclusion for all.

HOMEBOUND PUBLICATIONS

Since 2011 We are an award-winning independent publisher striving to ensure that the mainstream is not the only stream. More than a company, we are a community of writers and readers exploring the larger questions we face as a global village. It is our intention to preserve contemplative storytelling. We publish full-length introspective works of creative non-fiction, literary fiction, and poetry.

Look for Our Imprints Little Bound Books, Owl House Books,
The Wayfarer Magazine, Wayfarer Books & Navigator Graphics

WWW.HOMEBOUNDPUBLICATIONS.COM

BASED IN THE BERKSHIRE MOUNTAINS, MASS.

The Wayfarer Magazine. Since 2012, *The Wayfarer* has been offering literature, interviews, and art with the intention to inspires our readers, enrich their lives, and highlight the power for agency and change-making that each individual holds. By our definition, a wayfarer is one whose inner-compass is ever-oriented to truth, wisdom, healing, and beauty in their own wandering. *The Wayfarer's* mission as a publication is to foster a community of contemplative voices and provide readers with resources and perspectives that support them in their own journey.

Wayfarer Books is our newest imprint! After nearly 10 years in print, *The Wayfarer Magazine* is branching out from our magazine to become a full-fledged publishing house offering full-length works of eco-literature!

Wayfarer Farm & Retreat is our latest endeavor, springing up the Berkshire Mountains of Massachusetts. Set to open to the public in 2024, the 15 acre retreat will offer workshops, farm-to-table dinners, off-grid retreat cabins, and artist residencies.

WWW.WAYFARERBOOKS.ORG